The Country Friends® Collection

Parties

THE PARTY GURU:

Holly's Stress-Free PARTY PLANNING

RULE #1 You can never have too many **LISTS.**

RULE #2 Plan your **Menu.**

★ TRY TO SERVE MAIN COURSES YOU'VE MADE BEFORE & KNOW TASTE GREAT. EXPERIMENT WITH NEW DISHES WELL IN ADVANCE OF THE PARTY.

★ SERVE JUST 1 OR 2 APPETIZERS BEFORE A SIT-DOWN MEAL ~ YOU WANT YOUR GUESTS TO HAVE ROOM FOR THE MAIN EVENT! (SEE "DON'T" AT LEFT.)

★ BE AWARE OF FOOD ALLERGIES OR SPECIAL DIETARY NEEDS OF YOUR GUESTS.

★ COMPILE A GROCERY LIST FROM RECIPES SEVERAL WEEKS BEFORE THE PARTY.

#3 Think about the TABLE.

* IT SHOULD BE <u>FUN</u> TO SET ~ NOT A CHORE.
* SET IT A DAY OR 2 BEFORE THE PARTY. PUT OUT FRESH FLOWERS & PERISHABLES IN THE LAST FEW MOMENTS.
* DECIDE WHAT SERVING PIECES YOU'LL NEED ~ BEG OR BORROW FROM NEIGHBORS & FRIENDS IF YOU NEED TO!
* AFTER THE TABLE IS SET, SIT DOWN IN DIFFERENT CHAIRS TO GET A PERSPECTIVE FROM ALL LOCATIONS AROUND THE TABLE. MAKE CHANGES UNTIL YOU'RE SATISFIED.

RULE #4 Remember the Little Touches.

* MAKE SURE THE BATHROOM IS WELL-STOCKED WITH TOILET PAPER & GUEST TOWELS. A NIGHT-LIGHT OR SCENTED CANDLE IS A NICE TOUCH ~ BUT HOLLY RECOMMENDS NOT PUTTING A BURNING CANDLE ON THE BACK OF THE TOILET... YOU DON'T WANT SOMEONE'S PONYTAIL GOING UP IN FLAMES!
* KEEP LOTS OF ICE ON HAND FOR DRINKS.
* A SUPPLY OF LARGE TRASH BAGS WILL COME IN HANDY.

RULE #5 Keep it Simple & Have Fun!

A relaxed hostess is a happy hostess.
(repeat this mantra three times)

Summer White

…a beautiful way to host

Polish up your purty **handwriting**! Write out your invitation on a beautiful white card ~ buy the best quality you can in paper. Glue the card to a pretty white paper doily ~ let the lovely edges peep out behind the card. Hot glue on a tiny organdy or satin ribbon ~ or for a classic finish, use hot wax & a monogram seal to dress up your invitation.

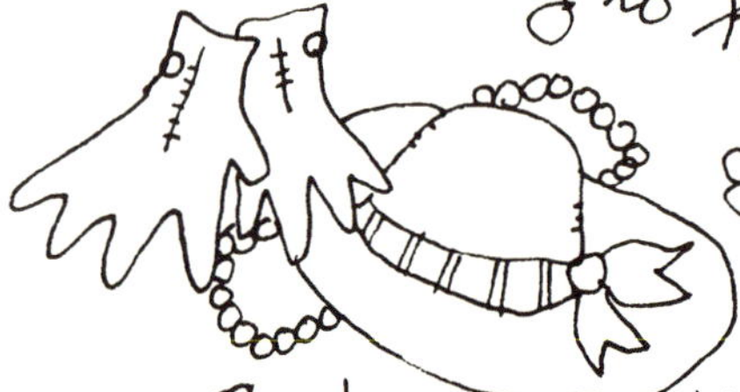

Guests come dressed in their very best **WHITES**… dresses, shoes, gloves & hats… very proper and very beautiful!

white pitchers look right: Fill them with a variety of all-white **flowers** in your table decorations ~ perhaps a loosely-arranged bouquet of **daisies, roses, cosmos, queen anne's lace**… pay a visit to your cutting garden!

Garden Party

a bridal or baby shower!

Use your best white china. Accessorize with charming white **fabrics**:

Drape the guest-of-honor's chair with white netting & ribbons.

- laces
- patterned netting
- organza
- all-white country quilts
- dotted swiss

Small boxes of chocolates tied up in several thicknesses of white tulle & satin ribbons make clever **favors**.

Tie on a tiny gold heart charm or trinket for a special touch.

♥ At Mary Elizabeth's baby shower, the Country Friends rolled white fabric napkins and pinned them with a silver-toned diaper pin for a clever table setting accent.

♥ antique-looking picture frames can double for name cards & menus... and guests will love to take them home as favors!

- ♥ Fresh Fruit with Dip
- ♥ Chilled Cucumber Soup
- ♥ Mixed Greens with Vinaigrette
- ♥ Herbed Salmon Puffs
- ♥ Steamed Asparagus
- ♥ Zesty Bread Sticks
- ♥ Fluffy Coconut Cake
- ♥ Champagne Punch

Herbed Salmon Puffs

2 c. canned salmon, skin & bones removed
1/2 c. fresh bread crumbs
3 green onions, white & green parts, finely chopped
1 T. lemon juice
1 T. melted butter
1 t. parsley
1/2 t. dried dill
1/4 t. salt
1/4 t. pepper
1 egg, beaten
1/2 c. milk

Mix all ingredients together in a bowl until well blended. Place in six well-greased baking cups. Set cups in pan of hot water. Bake at 350° for 45 minutes. Unmold puffs onto platter ~ garnish with fresh dill sprigs.

Zesty Bread Sticks

... cut into hearts for a shower!

1 1/2 loaves firm white bread, thinly sliced
2 sticks butter, softened
2 t. parsley
1 t. chives, chopped
1 t. tarragon
1 t. marjoram
1 t. garlic salt
2 T. sesame seed, toasted

Remove crusts from bread. Mix together remaining ingredients. Spread on bread slices. Cut bread into four sticks. Bake at 250° for 30 minutes. Turn off the heat; leave in oven for additional 40 minutes.

almost Champagne Punch

...a delicious non-alcoholic version!

2 (1 liter) bottles club soda, chilled
2 (1 liter) bottles ginger ale, chilled
6 c. unsweetened white grape juice, chilled

Combine ingredients in a large punch bowl. Serve in champagne glasses, and toast to the guest of honor!

The whole worth of a kind deed lies in the love that inspires it.

— THE TALMUD —

3 QUICKIE IDEAS FOR PARTY FUN

1. Celebrate a famous person's birthday ~

- ★ James Dean (Rebel without a cause)
- ★ ELVIS
- ★ Sean Connery (James Bond, 007 – licensed to party)
- ★ Katherine Hepburn
- ★ Cleopatra

2. THROW A WING DING!

Theme? Wings, of course! Serve lots of different chicken wings, from spicy BUFFALO WINGS to savory CHINESE CHICKEN WINGS. Serve 'em in metal buckets lined with red & blue bandannas. Decorate with anything chicken-related. Tuck a tiny feather in the invitation for fun!

3. Have a bunch over to watch Miss America on the tube ~ formal wear required, of course! A good excuse to break out the old bridesmaid dresses! Award prizes & tiaras to the best-dressed.

Feast Today

The Menu

- cream-filled cupcakes
- Lollipops
- bowls of jelly beans
- marshmallow pies
- lemon drops
- rock candy
- licorice whips
- peppermint sticks
- ice cream
- sprinkles
- chocolate syrup
- cherries
- whipped cream in-a-can
- chocolate-covered peanuts
- sugar cookies
- cream-filled sandwich cookies
- malted-milk balls
- peanut butter cups
- candy-coated chocolates
- divinity
- taffy
- cream-filled sponge cakes
- gumballs
- cotton candy
- peanut brittle
- fudge

For Tomorrow We Diet

Feast Today on every kind of candy & sweet you can dream of, at a party given by Kate, the perfect hostess for this occasion!

The Invitation: IT'S HALF THE FUN!

Find some small mailing tubes at the office supply store. Spray-paint them bright pink and then dot on brilliant spots of jelly bean-colored paint (or use stickers, if you like). Glue on a mailing label. Now on to the good part!

On bright pink paper, write out your party invitation (or make copies of our's below and fill in the blanks). Fold it up and insert in your decorated tube. Now put a hand.full of jelly beans & other hard candies in the tube, along with some licorice whips ~ when your guests open their invitations, they'll have a sweet surprise!

Feast Today For Tomorrow We

Join us for a Junk Food Feast
on

____

at ________ o'clock

hosted by ________________

at ____________________

D I E T

party decorations

...a feast for the eyes and the tummy!

Cover your table with a BRIGHT pink sheet, or maybe a POLKA·DOT one... we're talking colorful here. Let the sheet drape down and gather it around the legs of the table ~ tie with a BIG bunch of curling ribbons! Push a large lollipop down in the middle of the ribbon "bouquet" on each leg.

TRY NOT TO EAT THE TABLE DECOR BEFORE THE PARTY.

sweetie-pie Centerpieces:

SPRAY·PAINT A VINE CORNUCOPIA BRIGHT PINK & SPILL ALL KINDS OF CANDIES OUT OF IT, RIGHT DOWN THE CENTER OF THE TABLE ~ REALLY LOAD IT UP!

MAKE A HUGE NEST OF CURLING RIBBONS & PUT A GIANT FISHBOWL FULL OF BRIGHT JAWBREAKERS RIGHT IN THE MIDDLE OF THE TABLE.

MAKE AN EASY **GUMDROP TOPIARY!**

SUPPLY:

- CLAY POT ~ SPRAY·PAINTED WHITE
- STYROFOAM BALL & FOAM BLOCK
- DOWEL ROD
- GUMDROPS, HARD CANDIES
- HOT GLUE GUN

① assemble:

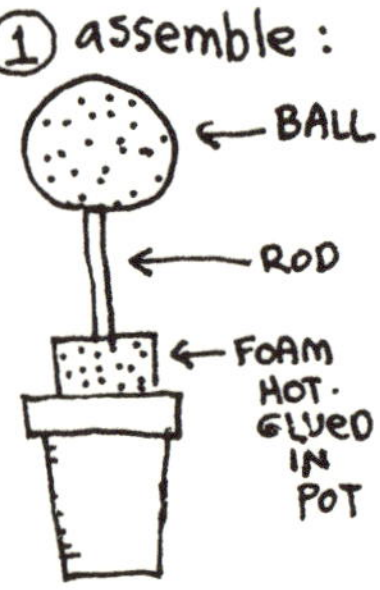

② NOW HOT·GLUE ALL KINDS OF HARD CANDIES & GUMDROPS ALL OVER THE BALL — COVER THE ENTIRE THING! WORK IN ROWS.

③ WRAP DOWEL ROD WITH LICORICE WHIPS.

④ HOT GLUE MORE CANDY ON POT.

Serve Your Feast

in clear bowls or on white dishes ~ let the beautiful colors of the candy

SHINE!

HAVE FUN!

There is a foolish corner in the brain of the wisest men.

~ ARISTOTLE ~

Moderation in all things.

- GREEK PROVERB -

IN THE UNLIKELY EVENT OF

Leftovers,

KATE SENDS HER GUESTS HOME WITH A PAPER TOTE BAG WITH A SILLY PINWHEEL TIED TO THE HANDLES WITH CURLING RIBBON STREAMERS. INSIDE, EACH PARTY-GOER WILL FIND A STASH OF SWEETS ... *and a little bottle of tummy-ache medicine!*

PARTY BLOOPER

As guests arrived for a party, I was trying to straighten up the kitchen counters. I grabbed a bag of cheese doodles and hid it quickly in the oven. Of course, I forgot about them as the evening progressed and I turned on the oven to heat up our meal ~ and of course, I found a whole bag of cheese doodles melted all over the oven 20 minutes later!

— Vickie —

SET A FESTIVE MOOD! THIS GET-TOGETHER BEGS FOR BRIGHT COLORS: Crepe paper streamers in alternating colors hung side-by-side across the ceiling ★ Balloons or tissue-paper flowers tied to the back of each chair ★ a piñata full of goodies ~ a centerpiece now, game later!

CHILI POT-LUCK

A GREAT PARTY FOR A CHILLY DAY!

Let the Fiesta begin!

CHILI FOR SUPPER CALLS FOR PLENTY OF PAPER NAPKINS! Make clean-up easy by covering your table with brown kraft paper; sprinkle on the confetti and add a handful of crayons, too, for some inspired doodling by your guests.

CHILI POTLUCK MENU

Re: THE CHILI

HAVE EVERYONE YOU'VE INVITED BRING A POT OF CHILI... POUR IT INTO ONE BIG POT, HEAT & SERVE. *Interesting!*

JoAnn's Guacamole Supremo

A REFRESHING STARTER DISH!

- 2 RIPE AVOCADOS, PEELED & CHOPPED
- 8-OZ. PKG. CREAM CHEESE, SOFTENED
- 1/2 C. SOUR CREAM
- 1 T. LEMON JUICE
- 1 T. MILK
- 5 DROPS HOT PEPPER SAUCE
- 1/4 t. GARLIC POWDER
- 1/8 t. SALT
- 1/8 t. PEPPER
- 1 LARGE TOMATO, SEEDED & CHOPPED
- 1 BUNCH GREEN ONIONS, CHOPPED
- 4-OZ. PKG. SHREDDED CHEDDAR CHEESE
- 1/2 C. BLACK OLIVES, CHOPPED

IN A BLENDER, COMBINE AVOCADOS, CREAM CHEESE, SOUR CREAM, LEMON JUICE, MILK, HOT PEPPER SAUCE, GARLIC POWDER, SALT & PEPPER UNTIL CREAMY & WELL-BLENDED. SPOON INTO A SHALLOW SERVING DISH ~ CHILL, NO LONGER THAN 48 HOURS. WHEN READY TO SERVE, TOP WITH TOMATOES, GREEN ONIONS, CHEESE & BLACK OLIVES. SERVE WITH TORTILLA CHIPS.

MARY ELIZABETH'S Nacho Cheese Biscuit Bread

PERFECT WITH A STEAMING BOWL OF CHILI!

- 10-OZ. CAN BISCUITS
- 1 T. MARGARINE, MELTED
- 3 T. CANNED GREEN CHILIES, DRAINED
- 1/2 C. SHREDDED MEXICAN CHEESE BLEND

PLACE 1 BISCUIT IN CENTER OF A LIGHTLY-GREASED BAKING SHEET. ARRANGE REMAINING BISCUITS IN CIRCLE AROUND CENTER BISCUIT. PRESS OUT INTO A 10-INCH CIRCLE. BRUSH WITH MELTED MARGARINE. TOP WITH CHILIES & CHEESE. BAKE AT 400° FOR 10-15 MINUTES OR 'TIL CHEESE IS MELTED & BISCUITS GOLDEN BROWN.

VICKIE'S SOUTH-OF-THE-BORDER LIME CAKE

BEAT THE HEAT AFTER DINNER WITH THIS DELICIOSO CAKE ~ SERVE WITH COOL, CREAMY FROZEN VANILLA YOGURT.

PACKAGED LEMON CAKE MIX
4-OZ. PKG. INSTANT LEMON PUDDING MIX
4 EGGS
1 C. VEGETABLE OIL
3/4 C. WATER
1/4 C. LIME JUICE

GLAZE:

2 C. POWDERED SUGAR
1/3 C. LIME JUICE
2 T. WATER
2 T. BUTTER, MELTED

IN A LARGE MIXING BOWL, COMBINE CAKE MIX, PUDDING MIX, EGGS, VEGETABLE OIL, WATER & LIME JUICE. BEAT FOR 2 MINUTES AT MEDIUM SPEED. POUR INTO GREASED & FLOURED BUNDT PAN. BAKE FOR 50 TO 60 MINUTES AT 350°. COOL IN PAN 20 TO 25 MINUTES. INVERT ONTO A COOLING RACK, REMOVE PAN & COOL ADDITIONAL 5 MINUTES. RETURN WARM CAKE TO PAN. USING A TOOTHPICK, POKE HOLES IN CAKE. COMBINE GLAZE INGREDIENTS ~ POUR OVER WARM CAKE. COOL COMPLETELY. INVERT ONTO SERVING DISH ~ SPRINKLE WITH POWDERED SUGAR. GARNISH WITH LIME SLICES & FRESH FRUIT.

¡Olé!

Only your real friends will tell you when your face is dirty.

-SICILIAN PROVERB

PARTY BLOOPER

I once hosted a dinner party; the food was perfect, the table looked gorgeous, I was jovial, vivacious, charming... & I had a large piece of black pepper between my two front teeth all evening. Lovely!

- Mary Elizabeth -

HOLLY'S

MOCK MARGARITAS

TASTES JUST LIKE THE REAL THING!

- 12-OZ. CAN FROZEN LEMONADE, THAWED UNDILUTED
- 12-OZ. CAN FROZEN LIMEADE, THAWED UNDILUTED
- 1 C. POWDERED SUGAR
- 6 C. ICE, FINELY CRUSHED
- 2 TO 3 DROPS GREEN FOOD COLORING
- CLUB SODA
- LIME SLICES
- COARSE SALT

IN A PLASTIC CONTAINER, COMBINE LEMONADE, LIMEADE, POWDERED SUGAR, ICE & FOOD COLORING. MIX WELL. COVER & FREEZE, STIRRING OCCASIONALLY. BEFORE SERVING, ALLOW MIXTURE TO THAW SLIGHTLY BY STANDING AT ROOM TEMPERATURE FOR 30 MINUTES. IN A BLENDER, COMBINE 2 CUPS OF MIX WITH 1 CUP OF CLUB SODA. BLEND 'TIL SMOOTH & SLUSHY. RUB GLASS RIM WITH LIME SLICE ~ DIP INTO COARSE SALT. FILL & GARNISH WITH LIME SLICE.

You must do a crazy thing once in a while to keep from going NUTS.

~ HARRY HIRSCHFIELD

COOKING with a CROWD: SUPPLY A PLAIN OR DECORATED APRON FOR EACH GUEST. ASSIGN EVERYONE A JOB & COOK UP SOME FUN! INVITATIONS CAN BE WRITTEN ON A RECIPE CARD ATTACHED TO A WOODEN SPOON.

to: Mary E. & Molly
Can't wait!
Please come to an All-Girl-All-Ages P.J. Party at Holly's House at 8pm ★ Friday
Bring your pillow & blankie for an evening of chick flicks and pizza!
P.S. Jammies and Bunny Slippers Required!
Count us in!
to: Kate & her Grandma
RSVP: yes!
to: Vickie
I'll be there!
to: JoAnn

the invitation:

one idea~

Cut out a pillow-shaped card & write your party details on it. Then slip it inside a little fabric pillowcase you've stitched yourself!

Paint your guest's name on the little pillowcase with fabric marker, and hand-deliver~in your jammies, of course!

another thought~

Buy inexpensive pillowcases at a discount store. Using fabric paint & markers, write your party invitation right on the pillowcase. Decorate it with a star-&-moon design (use ours, if you like)~ navy cases with gold & white paint looks dreamy! Roll the case up, tie with a ribbon & drop it in a mailing tube... then let the fun begin!

the menu:

pizza
fresh veggies
cold drinks
munchies

...trace our man-in-the-moon for your invitations if you like.

come in your P.J.s...

...All girls, All ages!

★ use PRE-BAKED PIZZA CRUSTS WITH THESE TASTY PIZZA IDEAS:

THREE★CHEESE CHICKEN PIZZA

¼ c. MARGARINE, SOFTENED
½ c. CHEDDAR CHEESE, GRATED
¼ c. FRESH PARMESAN CHEESE, GRATED
1 CLOVE GARLIC, MINCED
¼ t. DRIED ITALIAN SEASONING
1-½ c. COOKED CHICKEN BREAST, CHOPPED
1 c. MOZZARELLA CHEESE, GRATED
¼ c. RED PEPPER, CHOPPED
4 GREEN ONIONS, CHOPPED

....

COMBINE MARGARINE, CHEDDAR & PARMESAN CHEESES. STIR IN GARLIC & ITALIAN SEASONINGS & SPREAD ONTO PIZZA CRUST. TOP WITH REMAINING INGREDIENTS. BAKE AT 350° FOR 10 MINUTES.

CHEESY Tex-Mex PIZZA

1 LB. BULK SAUSAGE OR GROUND BEEF
SMALL JAR TACO SAUCE
1-½ c. CHEDDAR CHEESE, GRATED
1-½ c. MONTEREY JACK CHEESE, GRATED
LETTUCE, SHREDDED
TOMATOES, CHOPPED
BLACK OLIVES, CHOPPED
GREEN ONIONS, SLICED
SALSA
SOUR CREAM OR RANCH DRESSING

...

BROWN MEAT IN SKILLET. DRAIN GREASE. STIR IN TACO SAUCE. SPOON ONTO PIZZA CRUST ~ TOP WITH CHEESES. BAKE AT 400° FOR 10 TO 15 MINUTES. TOP WITH LETTUCE, TOMATO, OLIVE & GREEN ONIONS. SERVE SALSA, SOUR CREAM OR RANCH DRESSING ON THE SIDE.

HOLLY'S ALL-GIRL-ALL-AGES

P.J.s & Pizza

Make "Holly-wood" eyewear

... GLAMOROUS!

- SUNGLASSES
- ENAMEL PAINTS
- FABRIC PAINTS
- FAUX JEWELS
- GLITTER
- FEATHERS
- TINY STICKERS
- GLUE
- PAINTBRUSHES

...

LET EACH GUEST DECORATE THEIR SUNGLASSES WITH A VARIETY OF FUN DECORATIVE OBJECTS ~ EACH PAIR WILL BE UNIQUE!

WHAT'S A PARTY WITHOUT

GOODIE BAGS?

Holly filled one for each guest with:

- A disposable camera (lots of photo-funny opportunities at this party!)
- Pink foam hair-rollers (what looks sillier? A real ice-breaker)
- Little boxes of tissues (girls get weepy at movies)
- inexpensive sunglasses for "Holly-wood" eyewear
- Plain white PILLOWCASE
- a diary or small journal

Friendship Pillowcases

...autographs & messages you'll remember long past party-time!

SUPPLIES:

- PLAIN PILLOWCASES
- FABRIC MARKERS & PAINTS
- RUBBER STAMPS
- STAMP PADS
- IRON
- PAPER TOWELS

...

SET UP TABLE WITH SUPPLIES. PUT SEVERAL LAYERS OF TOWELS INSIDE PILLOWCASE TO PREVENT MARKER BLEED-THROUGH. DECORATE & SET WITH HOT IRON.

Party: no boys allowed!

Play the "Dear Diary" Game

Guests record in a diary their inner-most fantasies, a funny story from the past or something revealing about themselves. Each entry is numbered. Guests draw a number and read out loud that entry as everyone guesses who wrote it!

1. Mary Elizabeth 2. Holly 3. JoAnn 4. Kate 5. Vickie

CAN YOU MATCH

The COUNTRY FRIEND® with the TRUE CONFESSION?

A. "I am dreaming that Robert Redford & I are eating hot fudge sundaes. They are covered with whipped cream & chopped pecans & cherries. The fudge is sooooooo hot and there's a wickedly-rich brownie down under that creamy vanilla ice cream. Oh, give me more, more, more... and could I have another piece of cheesecake with that?"

B. "I think Richard Simmons is sexy."

C. "I always wanted to be a Rockette."

D. "I spilled baked beans down the front of my wedding dress."

E. "I fantasize about riding a bus ... Ricardo Montalban and I are the only passengers. Abraham Lincoln is the driver. I am wearing a fur coat and spike heels, and as we go through the toll booth, CENSORED

answers: 1-B 2-E 3-C 4-A 5-D

OTHER SLUMBER PARTY FUN:

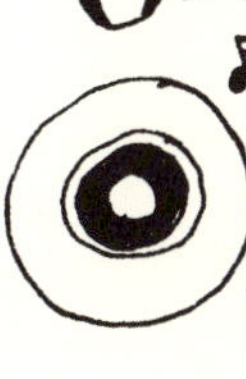

PLAY OLD SONGS. SING & DANCE!

PLAY WITH COSMETICS & MUD PACKS.

LOOK AT OLD YEARBOOKS.

GOSSIP!

WATCH "HUNK" MOVIES— anything starring Richard Gere or ELVIS or Keanu Reeves.

hjklom,elamdjeuqoajdkKLKASHDHWnk5690eroppr!#=½

A gReAT waY tO mEEt nEW fRienDS anD Catch UP on NeWs FrOM OLd FRIendS...

THrOW a PaRTy!

OUr MaKE A NEW FrieND Press PArTy wIll gEt You BAcK iN CIrcuLatioN... ANd ThAT'S tHe sCOop!

ewyurewornueorhedfuyiub¢*rjwerjniuMNB89*rieorer-../

The Invitations

Make 'em up to look like newspapers! Get out the old typewriter, use the computer, or just draw one up like Mary Elizabeth did.

Use your imagination ~ put photos of yourself, friends & celebrities in your paper; who's to say whether Pavarotti will be at the party? You never know!

Be sure to emphasize that each guest should bring a friend to the party.

Decorations

...Black & white, of course! Make a tablecloth from newspaper. Use scissors to scallop the edges if you like.

A clever centerpiece will be the "talk" of the party ~ Red flowers add zip to the black & white theme. You might put rolled-up papers in a canvas bag on the table, just like they're ready to deliver.

An old-time typewriter would also make a great table decoration ~ roll a copy of your invitation up in it. Place an old felt fedora with a "PRESS" card next to it. (THINK CLARK KENT.)

andkeworwerwpri¢*78TRm1()mnnfapoTBU90dforwerowrjkmmj

At the Door...

PASS OUT A NOTEPAD, PENCIL & "INTERVIEW QUESTIONS."... more about that later!

EACH GUEST CAN BE GIVEN A PRESS BADGE ...otherwise known as a nametag!

HOW TO MAKE PRESS BADGES:

1. Paint wooden ovals with white paint. Hand-letter the word "PRESS" across the top, leaving room for a guest's name.
2. Cut a sunburst design from heavy weight colored paper ~ glue onto the back of the wooden oval.
3. Add a wide strip of ribbon on the back of the oval ~ glue it on.
4. Glue pinbar backs on back-side of oval. Provide paint markers to guests so they can personalize their badges.

The Interview

A TERRIFIC ICEBREAKER! Guests use their notepads & pencils to "interview" the other party-goers using the list of questions passed out at the door. Some ideas:

- ✓ Find three people who love to garden.
- ✓ Who loves to cook? Who doesn't?
- ✓ Who's the most famous person you've ever seen in an airport?
- ✓ What's your favorite magazine?
- ✓ Which section of the paper do you read first?
- ✓ Find someone in the crowd who speaks French.

ndsabdsjrhwurowrbejfbsmn789340&*)(Ejkbnsdbsdwgrkwe5y

hejkaeisddbdfWEUGNB¢&(QwrjbM$6.srlkurlnmarfmadajfb,e

FOOD

Keep refreshments easy to serve ~ lots of appetizers & snacks will make front-page news.

NEWSROOM MUSHROOM DIP

1 LB. FRESH MUSHROOMS, SLICED
4 GREEN ONIONS, CHOPPED
4 T. BUTTER
2 · 8 OZ. PKGS CREAM CHEESE
½ t. SALT
1 t. WORCESTERSHIRE SAUCE
1 t. SOY SAUCE
TORTILLA CHIPS FOR DIPPING

....

SAUTÉ MUSHROOMS & ONIONS IN BUTTER IN SKILLET. ADD CREAM CHEESE & SALT, WORCESTERSHIRE & SOY SAUCE. COOK, STIRRING OFTEN, OVER LOW HEAT 'TIL CHEESE IS MELTED. SERVE WARM WITH CHIPS.

ENTERTAINMENT

PLAY

TYPESET

...A FUN VERSION OF SCRABBLE FOR A GROUP!

Using a 3-to-4 inch size alphabet pattern, trace several copies of each letter onto colored paper. Cut out letters. Place in a decorated box and mix 'em up. Pass the box around and let each guest pick a letter. Continue passing the box until all the letters have been picked. Guests have 5 minutes to spell their name. They may trade letters with other guests ~ that's where it gets wild & crazy!

FAVORS

...anything with a newspaper theme!

★ Roll up silly tabloids to send home ~ guests will enjoy reading about the birth of a 52-pound baby or the arrival of aliens.

★ Laminate the funny papers & cut into bookmarks.

w.547q4hjeNBQWDEUWtreuwir932==343.$*&nop)8,fkdlfrptk

I Scream You Scream Ice Cream PARTY

Menu

Ice cream & assorted toppings

*

Pecan shortbread cookie bowls

*

Banana Split Cake

*

Ice cream Cone Cupcakes

*

Coffee & Tea

NUTS & NOUGATS FUDGE FANTASTICKO MOCHA MINT

our invitations

look good enough to eat ~ almost! Buy some plastic foam balls that are about the size of a scoop of ice cream. Take 'em home & spray-paint 'em. (we like strawberry color, personally.) Ok now, hot glue those babies into some real flat-bottomed ice cream cones... one "scoop" per cone (unless that invitation is going out to a real glutton.)

All righty ~ now write out your invitation information on a long, skinny strip of paper. Fold it up accordian-style. Hot glue one end to the tip-top of the "scoop". Use a long straight pin to secure it all-folded-up to

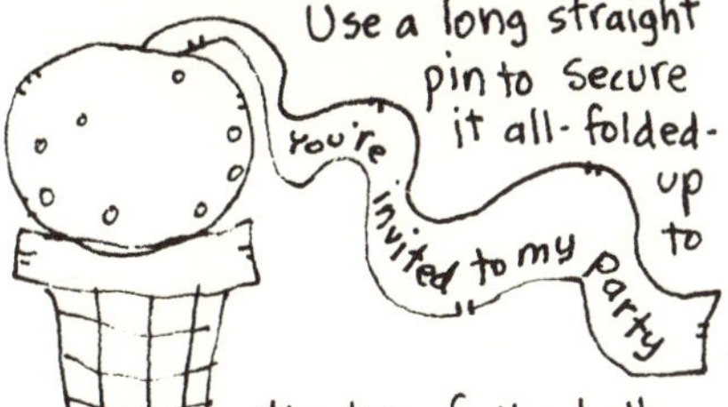

the top of the ball. (You might even put a big red bead on the pin for a "cherry"!)

Pack your invitation cones in empty ice-cream containers. Rent an ice-cream truck and drive it around, hand-delivering to your guests. (If that's not practical for you, we guess a minivan will do.)

STOCK UP WITH PLENTY OF

VANILLA ice cream

WITH ALL THE DIFFERENT FLAVORS OF VANILLA AVAILABLE TODAY, YOU CAN HAVE A CONTEST FOR THE WORLD'S BEST ~ THERE WILL BE NO SHORTAGE OF CONTEST JUDGES!

DON'T FORGET THE CHOCOHOLICS ON YOUR GUEST LIST... AND FOR THOSE STRONG SOULS WHO WILL STICK TO THEIR DIETS AT THE PARTY, OFFER SOME YUMMY FROZEN YOGURT.

★ TIP: SCOOP ICE CREAM INTO BALLS EARLY - PLACE IN DECORATIVE BOWLS, COVER WITH WRAP & FREEZE 'TIL PARTY TIME.

TRIPLE WHAMMY CHOCOLATE VERY VANILLA

DOUBLE FUDGE RIPPLE TANGY TANGERINE TWIST

BOYSENBERRY BLAST · PINEAPPLE ICE · SODA JERK'S SURPRISE · BROWN COW DELIGHT · TON O' CHERRY

toppings

anyone?

HOW ABOUT:

* HOT FUDGE, CARAMEL, PINEAPPLE, MARSHMALLOW & STRAWBERRY SAUCES
* MARASCHINO CHERRIES
* CRUSHED COOKIES & CANDIES
* CHOPPED NUTS
* SPRINKLES & JIMMIES
* BIG BOWLFULS OF WHIPPED CREAM

YES! YOU BET! OK! SURE! LAY IT ON!

pecan shortbread cookie bowls

1 1/4 C. FLOUR
8 T. BUTTER, SOFTENED
3 T. SUGAR
3/4 t. VANILLA
1/4 C. PECANS, FINELY CHOPPED

*

USING A FORK, BLEND TOGETHER FLOUR, BUTTER, SUGAR, VANILLA & PECANS UNTIL MIXTURE IS CRUMBLY. KNEAD DOUGH UNTIL IT HOLDS TOGETHER DIVIDE INTO 12 EQUAL PORTIONS PRESS DOUGH OVER INVERTED JUMBO MUFFIN PAN. LIGHTLY SPRAY PAN WITH NON-STICK VEGETABLE SPRAY FOR EASIER REMOVAL. PLACE ON BAKING SHEET, COOKIE SIDE UP. BAKE AT 350° FOR 10 TO 12 MINUTES OR 'TIL LIGHTLY GOLDEN. COOL SLIGHTLY & REMOVE CAREFULLY, USING POINT OF SHARP KNIFE TO RELEASE COOKIE BOWLS. COOL COMPLETELY ON WIRE RACK BEFORE USING.

CHOCOLATE BERRY · BUBBLE GUM

COFFEE & CREAM

DAQUIRI ICE

YUMMY WITH ICE CREAM!

banana split cake

2 STICKS MARGARINE, SOFTENED
1 C. SUGAR
2 EGGS
1/2 C. BUTTERMILK
1 C. BANANAS, MASHED
1 t. VANILLA
2 C. FLOUR
1 C. ROLLED OATS, QUICK-COOKING
1-1/2 t. SODA
1/2 t. SALT
6-OZ. PKG. CHOCOLATE CHIPS
1/2 C. WALNUTS, CHOPPED

*

CREAM TOGETHER MARGARINE WITH SUGAR & EGGS. BLEND IN BUTTERMILK, BANANAS & VANILLA. STIR IN FLOUR. ADD ROLLED OATS, SODA & SALT. MIX WELL. SPREAD INTO A GREASED 13" x 9" BAKING PAN. SPRINKLE WITH CHOPPED NUTS. BAKE AT 350° FOR 30 TO 35 MINUTES.

STRAWBERRY BINGE

ROOT BEER RAZZLE

CINNAMON RIPPLE

VANILLA CRUNCH

Kate's

ice cream cone cupcakes

...Kids love these!

1 Box cake mix
1 can frosting
18 flat-bottomed ice cream cones

Prepare cake mix according to instructions. Fill cones three-fourths full with cake batter. Place filled cones on a baking sheet ~ follow baking instructions for cupcakes on package. After taking out of oven, allow baked cupcakes to cool 20 minutes. Frost & decorate with sprinkles.

For extra credit:

Impress your party guests with this vintage soda jerk lingo:

- ★ **H**ouseboat (Banana split)
- ★ **M**ud (Chocolate Ice Cream)
- ★ **P**ink stick (Strawberry Ice Cream)
- ★ **G**o for a walk (Order to Go)
- ★ **P**air of drawers (Two Coffees)
- ★ **C**ity juice (Glass of water)

I need 2 white cows & a black stick, quick!

Fascinating

PARTY FAVORS

They Won't Forget

* Let your guests take home their name cards after the table is cleared; they'll love~

Potted herbs in clay pots

Little tiny Bird-houses or

Eggs in a nest

small Picture Frames

A big sugar Cookie with guest's name in icing

* Don't forget the child in all of us - We never really outgrow toys!

Rubber Duckies make great place cards at a baby shower.

Bubbles are fun at a garden party.

Squirt Guns will break the ice at a Backyard BBQ... so will Indian Head-dresses or Kid-size cowboy Hats on adult-size heads!

Wind-up Cars make table decor fun & fast... just line 'em up down the center of the table.

Plastic zoo Animals or Dinosaurs are great conversation pieces... be sure to get meat-eaters for your next party-at-the-grill.

Plastic Ants are funny favors at a picnic. Tie 'em up in white tulle with a black ribbon.

one word: Kazoos! (who can resist?)

A merry heart goes all the day.
- Shakespeare

PARTY BLOOPER:

"I spent several hours making the perfect dessert for a dinner party and remembered to bring it out ~ an hour after the last guest went home. AAARGH!" – JoAnn

Party Blooper:

"I invited everyone I knew to a New Year's Eve party and prepared enough food for an army... and wouldn't you know it? We had a blizzard and nobody came!"

– Holly

PARTY BLOOPER:

"At my son's birthday party, we made glow-in-the-dark tee shirts... and the kids spent the whole party inside the coat closet, looking at their shirts." – Mary Elizabeth

All's well that ends well.

~ old adage